EXPLORERS OF NORTH AMERICA

A TRUE BOOK

by

Brendan January

Children's Press®
A Division of Grolier Publishing
New York London Hong Kong Sydney
Danbury, Connecticut

Vikings, the first European visitors to North America

Visit Children's Press® on the Internet at:
http://publishing.grolier.com

Library of Congress Cataloging-in-Publication Data

January, Brendan, 1972–
    Explorers of North America / by Brendan January.
        p. cm — (A true book)
    Includes bibliographical references and index.
    Summary: Describes the activities of explorers in North America from 1000 to 1804 including Leif Ericsson, Christopher Columbus, Amerigo Vespucci, John Cabot, and Lewis and Clark.
    ISBN 0-516-21629-5 (lib. bdg.)   0-516-27195-4 (pbk.)
    1. North America—Discovery and exploration—Juvenile literature. 2. Explorers—North America—History—Juvenile literature. [1. North America—Discovery and exploration. 2. Explorers.] I. Title. II. Series.
E101 .J36 2000   24089145   9/00
970.01—dc21   99-058705

Contents

Leif Eriksson approaching "Vinland" (present-day Canada)

The First Explorers

Around A.D.1000, a Viking named Leif Eriksson made a daring journey. In a sturdy ship, he sailed west across the Atlantic Ocean. No one knew what lay ahead. After several weeks, Eriksson landed on the coast of what is today called Canada.

Eriksson called this place "Vinland."

Eriksson, who lived in northern Europe, was one of the first people from that part of the world to see North America. The Vikings built a small village in Vinland, but it failed. It was several hundred years before anyone repeated Eriksson's feat.

In the 1400s, explorers from Europe (a region made up of many different lands, including Italy, Spain, Portugal, France, and England) began an amazing period of discovery. The Europeans desperately searched for a sea route to the Indies (the area we call southern and eastern Asia today). These lands had tasty spices and magnificent cloth called silk. Europeans would pay heavily for these items. The country that found the route to the Indies would become rich.

Columbus's ships, the *Niña*, the *Pinta*, and the *Santa Maria*, on their way to the New World

In August 1492, Christopher Columbus tried to reach the Indies by sailing west across the Atlantic Ocean. The king and queen of Spain provided Columbus with three ships for his journey—the *Niña*, the *Pinta*, and the *Santa Maria*. After more than two months at sea, a member of the crew spotted a sliver of white beach. Land! Columbus named the island San Salvador, which is one of the islands in the

Christopher Columbus reaches one of the islands in the Caribbean Sea.

Caribbean Sea. Columbus returned to Europe and told everyone that he had found the Indies. He even called the people on the islands that he had visited "Indians."

How Was America Named?

Columbus may have found the Americas first, but they were named after another explorer—Amerigo Vespucci. Vespucci explored parts of South America. In letters he wrote, Vespucci claimed to have found a new continent. The story of his travels was published in 1507 and was read all over Europe. A German geographer printed a book of maps and decided to call the new land "America" after Amerigo Vespucci.

Amerigo Vespucci

The Search for Gold

News of Columbus's discovery excited the Spanish people in Europe. People were thrilled by his reports of gold, pearls, and jewels. In 1519, Hernán (or Hernando) Cortés led an army of six hundred men into what is today called Mexico. Armed with guns and protected by

armor, the Spanish conquered
the mighty Aztec Indian
empire. Ships loaded with gold
and silver returned to Spain.

Another Spaniard, Francisco Vásquez de Coronado, heard a legend of seven cities made from gold. In 1540, Coronado led about three hundred Spanish soldiers into what is today the southwestern United States. But instead of finding golden cities, Coronado dis-covered villages of mud bricks. Disappointed and angry, Coronado continued on. He and his men saw the towering walls of the Grand Canyon. In 1541, they journeyed east into

Although he did not find the riches he sought, Coronado did discover the Grand Canyon.

the vast Great Plains. They were stunned by the size of the massive buffalo herds. But after two years of searching, Coronado returned to Mexico a failure. He never found the cities of gold.

Hernando de Soto

Another Spaniard also searched North America. In May 1539, a Spanish nobleman named Hernando de Soto landed in Florida with six hundred men. For six months, he

De Soto and his troops spent six months wandering in Florida's forests and swamps like this one.

and his men searched for the glimmer of golden cities in the forests and swamps of Florida. They found nothing.

De Soto led his men north into what is today Georgia, North Carolina, and South Carolina. Hacking through thick forests and swamps, they traveled west into Alabama and Mississippi. In 1541, the party crossed the Mississippi River into today's Texas. By 1542, the men were exhausted, and de Soto died of fever. Only three hundred men survived the return journey to Mexico.

The Search for a Passage

The Europeans soon realized that Columbus had been wrong. North America and South America were not the Indies but a new land. Still, the Europeans dreamed of reaching the Indies for its spices and its other treasures. The Spanish searched the coast of

South America. Everywhere, they looked for a passage through the land to the Pacific Ocean. But none existed.

During the 1500s, the Spanish controlled the southern

Atlantic Ocean. Armed with cannons, their warships watched for any English or French ship that dared sail into their waters. The English and French explorers steered their ships north to

An English ship being attacked by the Spanish

avoid the Spanish. They dreamed of finding a route through North America to the Indies. They called this route "The Northwest Passage."

Today, we know that there is no Northwest Passage. Because of ice and land, it was almost impossible to sail through North America to the Pacific. But the Europeans were certain it existed. In searching for the passage, the Europeans explored North America.

The Ships

Most of the explorers' ships were less than 100 feet (30.5 meters) long and built from oak wood. Two or three masts poked up through the deck. The tallest one was called the mainmast. The sails were made of canvas, wool, or heavy linen. When the wind blew from behind the ship, the sails filled and pushed the ship forward. These ships could survive major storms.

Columbus traveled across the Atlantic Ocean in boats called caravels.

Cabot and Verrazano

In May 1497, John Cabot gathered a crew of eighteen men on a tiny English ship called the *Matthew*. Cabot planned to reach the Indies by sailing north across the Atlantic Ocean. On June 24, Cabot sighted land, probably what today is called Newfoundland.

John Cabot prepares to leave for his first journey with his son Sebastian in 1497.

The next year, Cabot led five ships on another voyage. No one knows exactly what happened on Cabot's second voyage, but most believe that Cabot was lost at sea.

The French also looked for the Northwest Passage. A French king hired an Italian sea captain named Giovanni da Verrazano. In January 1524, Verrazano set sail for North America. After six weeks, he sighted land that is today the coast of North Carolina. Far off-shore of North Carolina are long and narrow sandbanks. Looking past these islands, Verrazano saw water. He exclaimed that he had found the route to the Pacific Ocean.

Verrazano continued north and explored the coast of what is today Virginia and New Jersey. Then, Verrazano wrote of a "very pleasant place, situated amongst certain little steep hills." He had discovered New York Harbor.

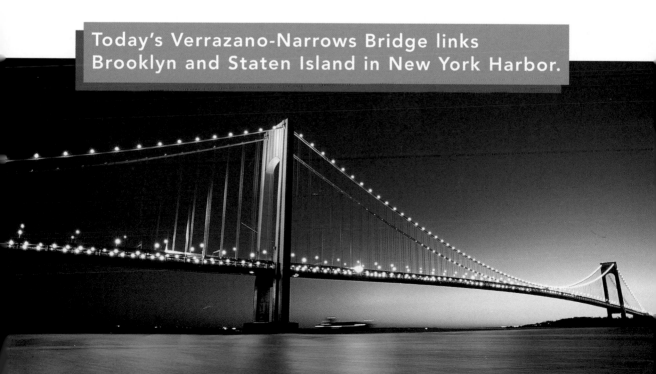

Today's Verrazano-Narrows Bridge links Brooklyn and Staten Island in New York Harbor.

American Indians in canoes swarmed around his ship. They traded beads for furs and food. Verrazano wrote that they were "the goodliest people, that we have found in our voyage." In June, Verrazano returned to France.

Cartier and Hudson

Verrazano's claim of a passage to the Indies was soon discovered to be false. A Frenchman, Jacques Cartier, decided to look for the passage farther north. In 1534, Cartier set sail with two ships and 120 sailors. They sighted the island of Newfoundland after twenty

days and then found the Gulf of St. Lawrence. The body of water led to a mighty river that flowed south. Cartier wondered if this could be the passage. The next year, Cartier returned to find out. In August

1535, he arrived at the mouth of the river and ventured in. As they sailed south, the river narrowed. Cartier left some of his ships behind and pressed on. By October, Cartier had

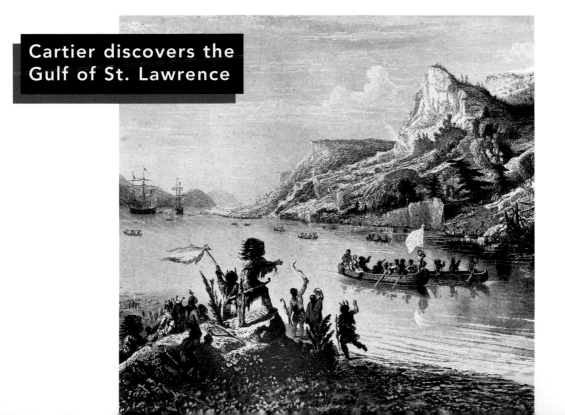

Cartier discovers the Gulf of St. Lawrence

journeyed more than 1,000 miles (1,609 kilometers). But rough water in the river blocked him. He could go no farther.

Years later, an Englishman named Henry Hudson was determined to try to complete Cartier's journey. Hudson believed that the passage must be even farther to the north. In 1607, Hudson ventured into the frigid Arctic Ocean. But food dwindled, and icy storms blasted his ship. He was forced to turn back. The next year,

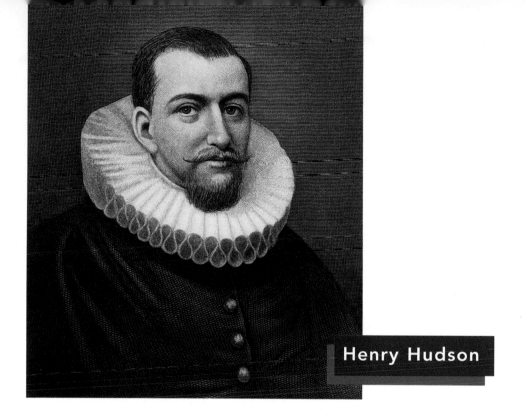

Henry Hudson

Hudson again pointed his ship north. Again, he failed to find a passage.

In 1609, Hudson sailed to Virginia and moved north. On September 11, Hudson entered New York Bay and discovered a beautiful, wide river. Excited, Hudson followed the river north for 150 miles (241 km). Today, the river still bears his name—the Hudson.

Hudson returned to North America in 1610. This time, he sailed far to the north and into a giant bay. Huge chunks of ice floated in the waters around him. Desperately, the crew steered the craft past dangerous ice floes that could have crushed the ship.

Hudson's ship, the *Half Moon*, on the river named after him—the Hudson River

In November, Hudson ordered the ship dragged ashore. The crew spent seven months waiting for spring. They were miserable. Food grew scarce, and howling snowstorms covered the landscape in snow and ice.

The area where Hudson disappeared is called Hudson Bay today.

In June 1611, the crew demanded to return to England. When Hudson refused, they forced him, his son, and seven others into a small boat and set them adrift. Hudson was never seen again. The body of water where Hudson disappeared is called Hudson Bay.

Into the Continent

By the 1660s, the French had built a colony in Canada. Two French-Canadians, Louis Jolliet and a priest named Jacques Marquette, heard stories from American Indians about a giant river. The Indians called it Mississippi, which means "big water."

Statues of Marquette and Jolliet adorn the Parliament building in Quebec, Canada.

In May 1673, Jolliet and Marquette paddled through the Great Lakes. They then carried their canoes overland to a stream that led to the Mississippi. The river's beauty and size awed the two men. They marveled to see people and animals that no

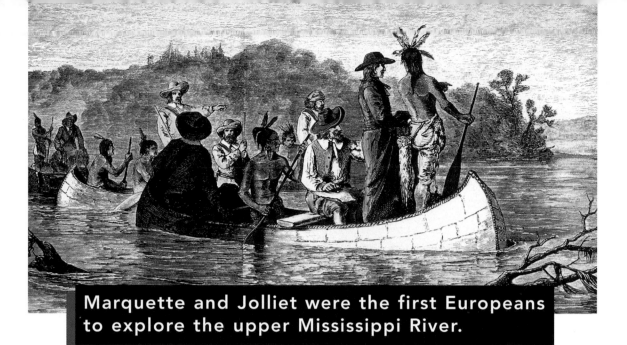

Marquette and Jolliet were the first Europeans to explore the upper Mississippi River.

person from Europe had ever seen before. They paddled their canoe into a catfish so large that the boat almost overturned. In mid-July, the men turned back at the spot where the Arkansas River joins the Mississippi.

Later, another French explorer, René-Robert Cavelier Sieur de La Salle, traveled on the Mississippi River. But he went farther than Jolliet and Marquette. In January 1682, La Salle led an expedition of fifty Frenchmen and American Indian warriors. With the strong current, they paddled down the Mississippi and reached the Gulf of Mexico by April. La Salle claimed the entire Mississippi River for France.

The land around the Mississippi remained French for more than

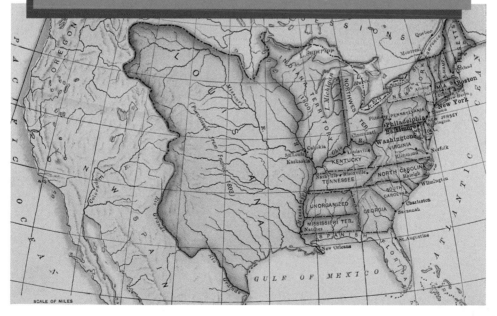

The Louisiana Territory stretched from the Mississippi River to the Rocky Mountains.

one hundred years. In 1803, Thomas Jefferson, president of the United States, bought the area from the French for $15 million. To learn more about this land, Jefferson sent two men, Meriwether Lewis and William Clark, to explore it.

Lewis and Clark left St. Louis in 1804. They traveled across the vast Great Plains, through the Rocky Mountains and finally reached the surf of the Pacific Ocean. They saw plants and animals (such as coyotes and prairie dogs) that they had never seen before.

Lewis and Clark explore the new United States territory.

Lewis and Clark also solved a mystery. They found that no river or sea could carry a ship through North America. The passage—the hope and dream of so many explorers—never existed.

To Find Out More

Here are some additional resources to help you learn more about explorers:

 **Books**

Fritz, Jean. **Around the World in a Hundred Years: From Henry the Navigator to Magellan.** Putnam Publishing Group, 1994.

Hynson, Colin. **Columbus & the Renaissance Explorers.** Barrons Juvenile Publishing, 1998.

Kemoun, Hubert Ben. **The Adventures of Great Explorers.** Barrons Juvenile Publishing, 1999.

Stefoff, Rebecca. **Accidental Explorers: Surprises and Side Trips in the History of Discovery.** Oxford University Press Children's Book, 1993.

Wilbur, C. Keith. **Early Explorers of North America**. Globe Pequot Press, 1996.

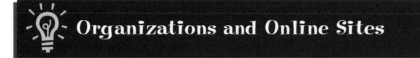

Organizations and Online Sites

A Confused Columbus
http://www.infoplease.com/ spot/columbus.html

This site investigates how Columbus incorrectly charted his own position on his four voyages to North America.

Henry Hudson and the Half Moon Replica
http://www.ulster.net/ ~hrmm/halfmoon/ halfmoon.htm

A biography of Henry Hudson and photographs of a replica of his ship is maintained in this site.

Hudson River Maritime Museum
One Rondout Landing
Kingston, NY 12401
http://www.ulster.net/ ~hrmm/welcome.html

The Lewis and Clark Trail
http://www.gorp.com/gorp /resource/US_Trail/LEWIS& CL.HTM

Follow in the footsteps of Lewis and Clark by reading about their expedition and exploring the Lewis and Clark National Historic Trail.

Important Words

colony group of people who travel to settle in another land but still obey the laws of their homeland

continent one of the great land masses on Earth

frigid cold, icy

gulf body of water

geographer a person who studies and maps features of the Earth's surface, such as mountains, oceans, and rivers

journey a long trip

legend story from the past that has gained wide belief

silk soft, rich cloth

spice something added to food to make it smell or taste different, such as cinnamon, pepper, and nutmeg

Index

Meet the Author

Brendan January was born and raised in Pleasantville, New York. He attended Haverford College in Pennsylvania, where he earned his B.A. in History and English. He earned his Master's degree at Columbia Graduate School of Journalism. An American history enthusiast, he has written several books for Children's Press, including *The Emancipation Proclamation, Fort Sumter, The Dred Scott Decision, The Lincoln-Douglas Debates,* and *The Assassination of Abraham Lincoln.* Mr. January lives in New Jersey.